W9-BWT-935

Step-by-Step Transformations

Turning Sap into Maple Syrup

Amy Hayes

Cavendish Square
New York

Published in 2016 by Cavendish Square Publishing, LLC
243 5th Avenue, Suite 136, New York, NY 10016

Copyright © 2016 by Cavendish Square Publishing, LLC

First Edition

No part of this publication may be reproduced, stored in a retrieval system, or transmitted in any form or by any means—electronic, mechanical, photocopying, recording, or otherwise—without the prior permission of the copyright owner. Request for permission should be addressed to Permissions, Cavendish Square Publishing, 243 5th Avenue, Suite 136, New York, NY 10016. Tel (877) 980-4450; fax (877) 980-4454.

Website: cavendishsq.com

This publication represents the opinions and views of the author based on his or her personal experience, knowledge, and research. The information in this book serves as a general guide only. The author and publisher have used their best efforts in preparing this book and disclaim liability rising directly or indirectly from the use and application of this book.

CPSIA Compliance Information: Batch #WS15CSQ

All websites were available and accurate when this book was sent to press.

Library of Congress Cataloging-in-Publication Data

Hayes, Amy.
Turning sap into maple syrup / Amy Hayes.
pages cm. — (Step-by-step transformations)
Includes index.
ISBN 978-1-50260-458-3 (hardcover) ISBN 978-1-50260-457-6 (paperback) ISBN 978-1-50260-459-0 (ebook)
1. Maple syrup—Juvenile literature. I. Title.

TP395.H39 2016
664'.132—dc23

2015010264

Editorial Director: David McNamara
Copy Editor: Cynthia Roby
Art Director: Jeffrey Talbot
Designer: Alan Sliwinski
Senior Production Manager: Jennifer Ryder-Talbot
Production Editor: Renni Johnson
Photo Research by J8 Media

The photographs in this book are used by permission and through the courtesy of: Pinkcandy/Shutterstock.com, cover; Daniel Loiselle/E+/Getty Images, cover; wsf-s/Shutterstock.com, 5; sianc/Shutterstock.com, 7; Oleksiy Maksymenko/Getty Images, 9; Amanda Lynn/First Light/Getty Images, 11; Jen Grantham/E+/Getty Images, 13; John Churchman/Photolibrary/Getty Images, 15; photosoup/iStock/Thinkstock, 17; Christopher Kontoes/Getty Images, 19; Sara Lynn Paige/Moment/Getty Images, 21.

Printed in the United States of America

Contents

First Step: Sap **4**

Transformation: Getting Hot ... **16**

Last Step: Maple Syrup **18**

New Words **22**

Index **23**

About the Author **24**

Syrup is made from sap.

Sap comes from **maple trees**.

5

First, a hole is drilled into a maple tree.

A **spile** is put into the tree.

9

Tubes are connected to the spiles.

Sap runs out of the tree and into the tubes.

11

The tubes run through the forest and into a **sugarhouse**.

13

At the sugarhouse, the sap will be turned to syrup.

15

The sap is sent to a **machine** that gets very hot.

The machine takes all of the water out of the sap.

17

When the water is gone, the sap becomes maple syrup!

18

19

Maple syrup is **delicious**.

21

New Words

delicious (de-LI-shes) Tasty.

machine (muh-SHEEN) Equipment with moving parts that is used to do a job.

maple trees (MAY-pul TREES) Trees that have sugary sap.

spile (SPYL) A spout inserted in a tree to draw off sap.

sugarhouse (SHU-gar-HOWS) A hut where the sap is turned into sugar.

Index

delicious, 20

machine, 16

maple trees, 4, 6

spile, 8, 10

sugarhouse, 12, 14

About the Author

Amy Hayes lives in the beautiful city of Buffalo, New York. She has written several books for children, including the Machines That Work and the Our Holidays series for Cavendish Square.

About BOOKWORMS

Bookworms help independent readers gain reading confidence through high-frequency words, simple sentences, and strong picture/text support. Each book explores a concept that helps children relate what they read to the world in which they live.

FREDERICK COUNTY PUBLIC LIBRARIES   NOV   2016   2 1982 02923 5888